I Love You Daddy, I Love You More

By

Vicki Addesso Dodd

Illustrations by Carolyn Justice

Book Design by Bonnie Molitor

The illustrations in this book were made with watercolor on paper.

ISBN-10: 0615696430
ISBN-13: 978-0615696430

Text copyright © 2012 Vicki Addesso Dodd
Illustrations copyright © 2012 Vicki Addesso Dodd

Published in 2012 by
Saratoga Springs Publishing, L.L.C.
Saratoga Springs, NY
SaratogaSpringsPublishing@gmail.com

All rights reserved. No portion of this book may be reproduced stored in a retrieval system, or transmitted in any form or by any means, mechanical, electronic, photocopying, recording, or otherwise without written permission from the publisher.

Saratoga Springs Publishing's books are available at special discounts when purchased in quantity for premiums and promotions as well as fundraising or educational use. Special editions can also be created to specification. For details, contact VADodd2@gmail.com.

This story is dedicated to my husband, Gregory and my father, Anthony (Tony) who both exemplify the true meaning of the word father.

Also, to my daughter, Kelsey, whose extraordinary love for her father inspired this story.

-Vicki

When I was a baby you held me tight.
You tucked me in and kissed me goodnight.

When I opened my eyes what did I see?
My big, strong Daddy looking over me.

I looked up at Daddy and thought to myself.....

I love you Daddy, I love you more.
I love you more than the day before.
With you as my Daddy and me as your girl,
anything's possible in this whole world.

As I got older and tried to crawl,
you stayed by my side so I wouldn't fall.

I pushed and pulled and then finally,
I crawled to my Daddy watching over me.

I looked up at Daddy and thought to myself.....

I love you Daddy, I love you more.
I love you more than the day before.
With you as my Daddy and me as your girl,
anything's possible in this whole world.

One day I stood up and took my first step.
I looked up at Daddy and then he just wept.

He held out his hand and said, "Come to me."
So I walked to my Daddy as he reached out for me.

I looked down at Daddy and thought to myself.....

I love you Daddy, I love you more.
I love you more than the day before.
With you as my Daddy and me as your girl,
anything's possible in this whole world.

I wanted to learn to climb a big tree,
so off to the park went Daddy and me.

As I reached for the tree he said, "It's OK, because right by your side your Daddy will stay."

I looked down and said,
"Will you always be there?
Will you always protect me
and show me you care?"

Daddy reached up to me
and held me in his arms.
He said, "With me as your Daddy
you will never know harm."

"With me as your Daddy and you as my girl,
anything's possible in this whole world."

I looked at my Daddy and said with a smile.....

I love you Daddy,
I love you more.
I love you more than the day before.

As the years go by
I'll remember that tree,
when all that mattered
was Daddy and me.

You'll watch me succeed

And give me away

*B*ut one thing is certain with each passing day......

I love you Daddy,
I love you more.
I love you more
than the day before!

Vicki Addesso Dodd is the author and coauthor of numerous groundbreaking medical publications, which she wrote as a research scientist at Columbia Presbyterian Medical in New York City. In 2004 Vicki, her husband, Gregory and her adorable Shiba Inu dog Sadie moved to Saratoga Springs to start a family. After the birth of her daughter Kelsey, she began to follow her passion, writing children's stories and decided to make her dream a reality.

Carolyn Justice studied Illustration at F.I.T. in New York City. She is now an accomplished pastel artist and instructor. Her work has been exhibited throughout the northeast and hangs in many private collections. She has three grown sons and lives in Saratoga Springs. This is her first children's book illustration and it is lovingly dedicated to her 5 grandchildren.

www.ingramcontent.com/pod-product-compliance
Lightning Source LLC
Chambersburg PA
CBHW040032050426
42453CB00002B/94